Desolate !
Beautif

Andros

D1648668

Ag. Pantelerimon (Dirt Rd. Desolate

Tinos in Greece

1. village AETOFOLIA -
2. KATO Kleisma   Church video
   Beautiful   Blue Dome

Greek Islands Travel Guide

3. Karkados
4. Kanowi   Small   Desolate

: Apagania .

ag Romanos
Beautiful
Uiou / beach
No parking

Dave Briggs and Vanessa Foudouli

Contents

1. Introduction to Andros and Tinos

The Greek islands of Santorini and Mykonos may be the bucket list destinations of choice for many, but it's the lesser known Greek islands that offer authentic experiences and laid-back moments. That's certainly the case for Andros and Tinos, two neighbouring islands that remain hidden gems when compared to their better-known Cycladic island counterparts.

Easily accessible within a few hours from Athens by ferry, Andros and Tinos combine rustic charm with contemporary chic. Both islands have great beaches, some incredible landscapes, and a completely different pace of life when compared to the conveyor belt tourism of Santorini.

Locally, Andros is a popular weekend break destination for Athenians, whilst Tinos is a major pilgrimage centre at certain times of the year for Orthodox Christians. Outside of Greece, these two islands remain mostly unknown.

In one way, that's a shame because both islands deserve more recognition. In another though, it's a great thing, because they both retain elements of what a real Greek island vacation is all about - beautiful beaches, great food, culture, history and a relaxed atmosphere.

In this guide, we'll introduce you to both islands, show you how to get there, and what there is to see and do. Whether you intend to spend your entire vacation on one or both islands, or prefer to use Andros and Tinos as stepping stones as part of your Greek island-hopping adventures, we hope you find this travel guide useful.

2. About this Travel Guide

This travel guide is one of a series of guides about Greece written by Dave Briggs and Vanessa Foudouli for their brand Real Greek Experiences. Unlike a surprising amount of travel guides out there, the authors have actually visited the places they write about! You can find out more about the authors in the author bio section.

The idea behind this travel guide, is to give you enough information to start planning a trip to Andros and Tinos, but you'll notice there's no set itinerary in this guide. The reason being that nothing quite beats getting out there and doing things yourself. What you will find though, is everything you need to discover the obvious (and not so obvious) highlights of these two fantastic Greek islands.

If you are interested in more information about planning a trip to Greece, the authors write regularly on their travel blogs.

www.davestravelpages.com

www.realgreekexperiences.com

You can also sign up for a useful series of free travel guides here:

https://www.davestravelpages.com/greece-travel-guides

3. Andros and Tinos at a Glance

Where: Andros and Tinos are two of the lesser known (to foreign visitors at least!) Cyclades islands in Greece. They are just a couple of hours away from Athens, and just a short ferry ride away from Mykonos.

Why Visit: Both Tinos and Andros boast lovely beaches, quaint villages, great hiking paths, fantastic food and an authentic, laid back atmosphere. Does that sound like your type of thing?

Currency: Euro

ATMs: Main towns Language: Greek, English spoken widely

Country Code: +30

Mobile Phones: Good reception all over the islands

Wi-Fi: Available all over the islands in hotels, tavernas and coffee shops. Digital nomads might want to make sure they have plenty of data to tether from their phones just in case.

High Season: July and August, also Greek Easter

Best Time to Visit: September

Accommodation: Ranging from camping to 5-star hotels with pools. Most accommodation is somewhere in between.

I Can Only Visit One: Tinos

What Aren't You Telling Me?: Meltemi winds. See the "When to go" section for more.

Bottom Line: Compared to Mykonos, Andros and Tinos are twice as nice for half the price!

4. How to Get to Andros and Tinos

Like many other Greek islands, Andros and Tinos do not have airports, so the only way to get there is by ferry.

Andros is only accessible by ferry from Rafina port. Tinos can be reached from either Rafina or the better-known Piraeus port.

Rafina is the lesser known port of Athens, but it's also smaller, friendlier, and much easier to get around than the larger Piraeus Port. In addition, Rafina is just a half hour away from Athens International Airport. If your flights are timed just right, you could land at Athens Airport, and be on a ferry to Andros or Tinos within a couple of hours!

Ferry Departures from Rafina to Andros and Tinos

There are a number of ferries departing on a daily basis from Rafina to Andros and Tinos. Most (if not all) of these ferries include both Andros and Tinos on the same route as the islands are quite close to one another.

Andros would be the first stop taking up to two hours to reach, whilst Tinos would be another one to two hours further on. Some ferries would then continue on to Mykonos or other islands in the Cyclades group.

Types of Ferry Available

There are various companies plying the route from Rafina to Andros and Tinos, and you'll sometimes find these leave within a half hour of each other. These companies operate different kinds of ferries, ranging from the faster High Speed ferries to slower boats.

While a high-speed ferry can take just over an hour to get to Andros, the larger ferries will take a couple of hours. If you are pushed for time you can get the high-speed ferry, however our preference are the larger, slower ferries. Since the trip is no more than 2 hours long to Andros, you will barely feel it. If you are going directly to Tinos, you might prefer a quicker boat.

Most of the ferries to Andros and Tinos can take vehicles on board. So, if you are planning a road trip in Europe or Greece, you'll find it easy to take your own car or campervan.

If you are hiring a car in Greece, it would be cheaper to hire it on arrival at each island to avoid paying the extra ferry ticket for the vehicle. What's more, certain car rental companies don't allow the transporting of their cars by ferry. See more in our "How to Get Around Andros and Tinos" sections.

Ferry Departures and Timetables

While many boats depart early in the morning, there are also evening options. Schedules tend to change between seasons, and also from year to year.

Booking Greek ferries can be a challenge for the uninitiated, but we've made it easy by having two in-depth guides that show you how.
https://www.davestravelpages.com/how-to-get-to-andros-greece-rafina-andros-ferry/

And
https://www.davestravelpages.com/rafina-to-tinos-ferry/

Tips for Using the Ferries in Greece

If you haven't used the Greek ferries before, here are a few tips to make your journey more pleasant!

Depending on the ferry you choose to travel on and your type of ticket, you may or may not be allocated a seat as a foot passenger. If you are travelling in the deck category, you won't have an allocated seat. In this case, get on the ferry early and find a place in the public areas as quick as you can!

Travel is quite smooth, especially on the larger ferries. If you are prone to seasickness and are travelling on the smaller, faster boats, you might as well take some seasickness pills.

If you're driving your vehicle on board, be prepared for lots of shouting and arm gestures as the staff try to get everyone loaded on board super-quickly.

Whilst food and drink are available on board, you'll find it cheaper to bring your own.

At busy times of the year, ferries can get quite crowded. Take that into account when you are getting ready to disembark. You will then get a taste of the Real Greece!

5. When to Go to Andros and Tinos

The best time to go to Andros and Tinos depends on what type of vacation you are after. Both islands have wonderful beaches if you're looking to soak up some sun, which makes summer the most popular season to visit.

Touring around, sightseeing, hiking, exploring, and tasting the delicious Greek food can be done at any time of year though. If you're flexible, early autumn is perhaps the best season.

Andros and Tinos in Summer

Most people choose to visit Greece in summer, and of course the Greek beaches are best enjoyed when the weather is warm.

If you've only been to Athens or the mainland, you may be pleased to know that the Cyclades islands typically have lower summer temperatures in comparison. Still, Tinos and Andros are pretty warm by any standards. Temperatures can easily climb above 30C / 86F on the warmer days, making the sea the perfect temperature to go swimming.

If your main aim is to hit the beaches, the best time to visit Andros and Tinos is in summer or early autumn. You do need to be aware of the Meltemi winds though. These are strong northern winds which are prevalent around the Cyclades islands in summer. More on this below.

Should you Avoid August?

August is a fairly busy month on both islands, just like on pretty much every other Greek island. Andros is particularly popular with Greek families during this month, as it is very close to Athens and ferry tickets are cheap in comparison to most other islands.

Tinos celebrates one of the most important Greek religious days, the Assumption of the Virgin, on the 15th of August. Thousands of pilgrims come from every corner of the Orthodox world to pay their respects. As a result, the island gets super busy for a few days before and after. If you are planning to visit Tinos around that time, make sure you book your accommodation and ferry tickets well in advance.

What Are the Meltemi Winds?

If you've been to the Cyclades before, you will have heard (or experienced!) the Meltemi winds. These strong northern winds are fairly seasonal, generally lasting from July to August, and occasionally in the early days of September.

Andros and Tinos are two of the islands which are most affected by the Meltemi winds. In fact, the area between Andros and Evia island to its north has some of the strongest winds in all of Greece!

On particularly windy days, many of the north facing beaches may not be as relaxing as you hoped. The winds will blow up the sand, and create waves that make it difficult, or even dangerous, to swim. On these days, avoid the northern beaches altogether and go to the ones on the south instead. Also, bear in mind the fairly strong currents in the Aegean.

Ask at your hotel where they think the best protected beaches are. As Andros and Tinos are quite big and have tons of beaches each, you will always find a quiet spot to put your towel and go for a swim.

Whilst Andros and Tinos are not nearly as busy in August when compared to Santorini or Mykonos, you should be prepared for more people than usual. In addition, hotel prices may be bumped higher for this season. Still, they will be very affordable - nothing like the peak season prices of caldera-view suites in Santorini!

Visiting Andros and Tinos in the Off-season

Unlike the most popular islands such as Santorini, Mykonos and Rhodes, Andros and Tinos have a rather short tourist season, which is basically July and August. Even early September isn't considered "the tourist season" anymore, and many family hotels close down after mid-September.

That is not to say, however, that you won't find anywhere to stay. You can always find accommodation, and it's totally worth visiting Andros and Tinos in the off-season. You will then find what most visitors are after – the authentic, Real Greece.

Things to Do in Spring and Autumn

Apart from the beaches, both Andros and Tinos have some pretty amazing hiking paths. Most people would find summer temperatures way too hot to go on long hikes around the Cyclades, so if your main aim is to hike, it's best to visit during spring or early autumn instead.

In terms of nature, the Cyclades are beautiful in spring, even though they are not the greenest of islands. Both Andros and Tinos will take you by surprise with their pretty, varied landscapes. Note that swimming may not be possible in spring, as the sea will still be too cold for most people.

If you are looking for a unique experience, you could consider visiting Andros and Tinos during Greek Easter, when the villages come alive with the local traditions.

Easter in Tinos and Andros

Most people try to avoid visiting Greece during Greek Easter, as the tourist attractions are closed for a few days. Very few people plan their travels around the most important religious and cultural event in Greece.

You should aim to experience the Greek Easter once in your lifetime, as it's really special. There are many Easter-related customs in Greece, and visitors thoroughly enjoy Greek Easter traditions, especially the culinary ones.

If you happen to be on either island for Easter, you are bound to have a blast. While a lot happens in the main towns, it's worth heading to the smaller villages to observe the Epitafios processions and Easter masses. As Tinos is an island of great religious significance, Easter is particularly important here, and is celebrated accordingly.

You can read more about Greek Easter traditions here
https://realgreekexperiences.com/greek-easter-traditions

6. How Long to Spend in Andros and Tinos

This is always a tough question to answer! Certainly, you'll find plenty of people who recommend visiting Andros for just a couple of days, but this is because it's a popular weekend break destination for Athenians. So really, it will come down to how long you have got, and what you like to do.

You could probably see all the "must sees" with three days on each island. Greek island hoppers might just spend a night or two on each island, whilst beach lovers may never want to leave! Hikers, on the other hand, could easily spend weeks on either island.

We'd say to allow at least two nights on each island to make your journey and experience worthwhile. If you find yourself in a position of choosing to spend more time on one island than the other, then make it Tinos. If you can only visit one of the islands, we'd also say to make it Tinos. That is not to say that Andros isn't worth it - so if you only have a day or two you can always visit Andros, which is a bit faster to get to. Either way, you won't be disappointed!

Our opinion

We visited Andros and Tinos for a late summer vacation. Our aim was to get some beach time and explore what the islands had to offer.

From our experience, we thought that 5 days in Andros and 6 days in Tinos was about right, although we could have easily stayed longer on either island! It really depends on how much time you have and why you are visiting Greece.

7. Andros Island Travel Guide - Map

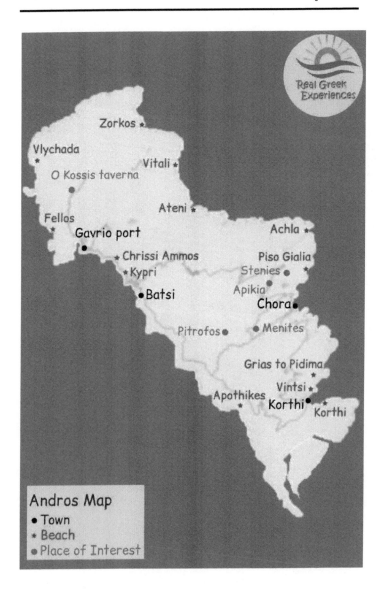

8. Introduction to Andros Island

Location: Cyclades Island Group
Population: 10,000 (approx)
Capital: Andros Town / Chora (Άνδρος / Χώρα)
Ferry Port: Gavrio
Hospital: Health Centre of Andros, Chora, Tel 22823-60001
Police: Chora, Tel 22820-22300

Andros is one of 26 inhabited islands in the Cyclades island group in Greece. With a permanent population of nearly 10,000 people, and an area of 380 square kilometres, it is the second largest Cycladic island after Naxos.

Whilst higher profile Cycladic islands such as Mykonos and Santorini draw people in from around the world, Andros has somehow flown under the radar of foreign visitors to Greece. It's certainly well known to Greeks though, as it makes an ideal weekend break getaway from Athens, being just a 2 hour ferry ride.

So, what can you expect in Andros?

It's really a mix of everything. Sophisticated chic, rustic charm, perfect beaches and untamed countryside. Throw in miles of hiking trails, medieval villages, and a proud history, and you have a destination with a great deal more soul than the more famous Santorini.

This guide will show you where to stay and places to visit in Andros. Whether you spend just a couple of days on the island, or stay for a week, there's plenty to do!

Don't Leave Andros Without Seeing

- Andros Town, also known as Chora
- The Statue of the Unknown Sailor in Chora
- Museum of Contemporary Art in Chora
- Panagia Thalassini Church in Chora
- The Old Lady's Jump (Grias to Pidima) Beach
- The Olive Oil Museum in Ano Pitrofos
- Stenies Village
- Taverna "O Kossis"

---

9. Where to Stay in Andros

Whether you plan to visit for a short break, or take a longer vacation, you'll need to find accommodation. Where to stay in Andros largely depends on what you want to get out of your holiday. Andros has a lot to offer – lovely beaches, hiking trails, dramatic landscapes and a lot of ancient and contemporary culture.

You can choose your accommodation in Andros according to the amount of time you have there, how you plan to get around the island, and what you would like to do during your holiday. This section breaks down the various areas.

For an interactive map on where to stay in Andros, visit:

Note: If you are visiting in the Meltemi season and swimming is important to you, you might consider staying at a hotel with a pool. Even though it's always possible to find a relatively quiet beach, you might have to drive a lot to reach it, which isn't for everyone.

Hotels in Batsi

A small coastal resort town, Batsi (or Mpatsi, or Batsion) is where many people choose to stay in Andros. While a lot of it closes down in winter, it is fairly lively in summer, and there is plenty of accommodation to choose from. If your main priority when you are visiting Andros is to go to the beach, and you also want a bit of nightlife, our advice is to stay in Batsi town.

A recommendation for budget self-catering accommodation is *St George Studios & Apartments*. The real bonus of staying here is the owner Christos, a young, enthusiastic guy who will offer plenty of information about Andros and suggestions on places to visit on a day to day basis. They also have the slightly more upmarket *St George Village* nearby.

Close to the beach, *Hotel Chryssi Akti* is a newly renovated 3-star hotel. There's a pool for guests to enjoy on those windy days, and its unique position means it's a short walk to tavernas and bars at night.

The **Blue Dolphin Guesthouse** has great views over the beach and offers good value for money. It's perfect for people who prefer Bed and Breakfast style accommodation, and the owner is able to recommend hiking in the area. Pick up from the port might also be available if you ask.

Hotels between Batsi and Gavrio Port

If you want to be on the beach but would prefer something quieter, you could stay at one of the areas between Gavrio port and Batsi town. Agios Petros and Agios Kyprianos both have lovely beaches, and there are also a few tavernas nearby. **Villa Maniati** has good ratings, great views, a welcome basket, and a breakfast guests seem to enjoy.

Note: We would not suggest staying at Gavrio port itself unless you have a vehicle, as you would still need to drive to a beach somewhere. However, you can spend a couple of hours here for a coffee or a drink. Gavrio offers fewer options for food and nightlife than Batsi.

Hotels in Chora Andros

If beaches are not your main interest, the best place to stay in Andros is probably Chora, the main town. If you thought that you may have seen the name "Chora" before, you are absolutely right. Most main towns on the islands are named Chora, which literally means "country" in Greek.

Located about an hour's drive from Batsi, the Chora is a really picturesque town. If you are staying in Andros for several days, you could consider splitting your time between Batsi and Chora to avoid a lot of driving.

If you want to be right in the middle of everything, you can't go wrong with **Micra Anglia Hotel**. Located close to the museums, this boutique hotel and spa is the perfect place to stay in Chora Andros, although it does have prices to match. Looking for an extra touch of indulgence? You should check out their suites!

Beachfront **Pension Stella** on Niborio beach is a good choice for people who want a personal touch. You could also walk to Stenies from here quite comfortably.

Hotels in Korthi

For people who want to escape everything, staying at Korthi bay could be a good choice. Korthi town itself is very quiet, and there are a few tavernas and cafes to choose from. The town has a long sandy beach that is fairly protected from the wind, as well as a smaller cove where many of the locals go. The famous Grias To Pidima beach is quite close by.

There are a few buses daily to both Gavrio and Chora, but if you decide to base yourself in Korthi you will be better off renting a car. **Nicolas Hotel** is one of the best options in Korthi, and there is also a pool, if it's too windy to go to the

10. How to Get Around Andros

Andros is a fantastic place to explore. With plenty of beaches, great hiking trails and a few interesting museums, there's lots to see and do, but you'll need to get around the island to see it.

Getting around Andros by Car

If you want to be independent, the best way to get around Andros is by car. You'll quickly get used to driving on the narrow, winding roads. Just take it at a nice steady pace, and let the locals who literally know every little curve of the road do their own thing. Which normally involves overtaking you!

Rent a Car in Andros

There are plenty of places to rent a car in Andros, mainly close to Gavrio port and in Batsi. Prices depend on the season, and it doesn't hurt to bargain, especially if you are booking the car on the spot. You might find that some of the big companies such as Hertz are represented on the island if you look online, but most likely the local companies are the best choice.

If you do a quick search, you will discover plenty of companies, such as Avance, Captain's Holidays, Bycar and Escape in Andros. We've no specific suggestion to make, so let Google be your friend when you come to search online!

Or, just rock up on the island and ask around - this often achieves lower prices. If you are specifically interested in an automatic car, it might be best to reserve in advance.

Before you travel, check if you need an International Driving License to drive in Greece. While some companies might not ask for it, you won't be covered in case of an accident unless you have a valid International Driving License.

Driving in Andros

While most of the roads in Andros are paved, there are long stretches of dirt roads. If you want to head to some of the more popular beaches in the north like Zorkos, Vitali and Ateni, it may be best to rent a 4WD.

If you rent a regular car, insurance will typically not cover you on dirt roads, so think about it before you decide. Check with your car rental company in regard to areas on the island your insurance will and will not cover you for.

Getting around Andros by ATV or Motorbike

Another way to get around Andros is by motorbike or ATV. You will need a valid driver's license if you want to rent any of these in Greece. While ATVs are very popular, especially with younger visitors, it's best to be cautious, as they are apparently quite easy to turn over. Also, if you decide to rent an ATV or motorbike, remember to use sunscreen, and don't forget your legs!

There are many companies on the island offering good quality bikes and ATVs, such as Dinos in Batsi town and Odysseas in Gavrio port.

Getting around Andros by Bus

Like most of Greece, Andros has a dedicated local bus service, with buses going to a few places around the island. The buses are called KTEL, and they are a fairly inexpensive way to see some parts of the island.

The bus network is not very extensive, as it only covers the biggest towns and a few of the beaches in Andros. The daily service between the port of Gavrio, the seaside town of Batsi and the picturesque Chora is fairly frequent, while buses to and from Korthi only run twice a day.

As you would expect, if you want to reach the smaller villages or the most remote beaches, you will need to find an alternative way to get around Andros. Whilst researching for this guide, we actually gave a couple of people hitchhiking from the beach a ride on one day!

Also, note that there are no buses after it gets dark. If you are staying at Batsi but want to go out at Chora or Korthi for the evening (or vice versa), you will need to find another way to return to your hotel.

Getting around Andros by Taxi

Some people may prefer to go around Andros by taxi. There is a taxi service located in Batsi, and a good starting point is Yiannis the driver who is friendly and polite. You can reach him at 22820-41081 or 6945-351079.

As an indication of costs, a ride from Batsi to Chora was 30 euro at the time of writing. If you are staying in Batsi and want to spend a whole day in Chora, you can get there on the KTEL bus and ask for a late evening taxi service.

Getting around Andros by Bicycle

Cycling around Andros would be a bit of a challenge in summer, with 30 degree temperatures not being uncommon, and strong winds. The island is also quite mountainous, so it would probably not be for beginners. Still, it would be great to cycle around Andros in spring or autumn.

Getting around Andros on Foot

Andros is a lovely island to walk and hike around. There is an extensive network of 180 kms of hiking trails and paths that are very well marked, covering most of the island. In fact, there is an annual walking festival in Andros, happening in October.

With average temperatures peaking at 21-22 degrees at that time of year, the weather should be very pleasant to hike around Andros. In the summer though, you'd need to think twice about covering long distances on foot. You can read more about hiking in Andros in the relevant section below.

Getting around Andros by Boat

Stef Lines, run by George Stefanou, organize cruises from Chora to Achla beach on small local boats. These run on a daily basis, depending on how strong the Meltemi wind is. If you are in Andros during peak season, it's best to reserve in advance. You can find more information on their FB page https://www.facebook.com/StefLinesAndros/

There are also other local boats running less popular routes from Batsi and Gavrio. Ask around for the most recent information.

Final Thoughts

Renting a car offers more flexibility and you will be able to explore more of the island. However, if you don't feel like driving on a Greek island, you can use the buses and taxis, or perhaps take a tour to get a local perspective. Whatever you decide, Andros won't disappoint!

You can read more about driving in Greece here https://realgreekexperiences.com/driving-in-greece-essential-tips-on-greek-driving-from-a-local

11. Villages and Places of Interest in Andros

The towns and villages in Andros add to the beauty of the island. Most people visiting Andros will take the trip to Chora and Batsi (if they aren't already staying there), but there are plenty of others as well, scattered all around the island.

At the same time, Andros has a fair few places of interest, such as natural wonders and castle ruins. It's an unusually green Cycladic island, with lots of springs and trees all around.

Chora Andros

Chora, literally meaning "country", is the main settlement in Andros, and it is pretty much the only town that is somewhat lively year-round. It's located on the east side of the island, and may be marked on Google maps simply as Andros.

Some people choose to stay in Chora when in Andros and so will have ample time to look around. Those who are staying elsewhere in Andros, should definitely make at least one day trip to explore this picturesque little town.

There are some lovely mansions, and the famous whitewashed Cycladic houses are everywhere. You can also see the ruins of the Venetian castle, which was built in 1207 and bombed during WWII.

Statue of the Unknown Sailor in Chora Andros

The impressive Unknown Sailor's statue in the large square is a symbol of Andros, and most Greeks will instantly recognize it. The statue was constructed in 1959, in honour of all the sailors who left Andros, but were lost at sea and never returned.

We were quite impressed to find out that the strong winds had brought it down in 2001, though it was later repaired and put back on its pedestal.

Chora is home to several museums, and if you want to see them all you would need to spend at least one full day.

Check the museum section in this Andros island travel guide for more information. Note that most museums are closed one day a week and during the afternoons.

After you've visited the Contemporary Art Museum in Chora, make sure you walk down to the beach. There's a lovely little church there, Panagia Thalassini, and the views are great! Also, check out the Tourlitis lighthouse, apparently the only lighthouse in Europe built on a rock. If you are there on a windy day, you will literally be blown away!

There are plenty of tavernas and cafes on the main street, so you can take a break from all the sightseeing and watch the world go by. You will instantly feel that Chora has a lively local community – we saw many people greeting each other and sitting for a coffee. There is also a popular outdoor cinema, showing different movies every night.

Note that if you are driving into Chora, you will have to park in the designated parking area right outside the town.

Batsi Town

Batsi is a small coastal resort town on the western side of the island, a short drive south from the port of Gavrio. It may be marked as Mpatsi or Batsion on Google maps - apparently it's all Greek to Google as well! Batsi is especially popular with Greek families, due to its protected bay.

Unlike Chora, the town itself doesn't have many attractions. However, it's a good base if you want to explore the western beaches, as there are many tavernas, cafes and rooms to rent. There is also an outdoor cinema, showing a different movie every night.

Even if you aren't staying in Batsi, you could spend a few hours for a coffee or a meal on the picturesque promenade, and maybe even take a swim. In terms of tavernas, we tried *Mi Se Meli* and *O Stamatis*, and they were both fine.

Between Batsi and Gavrio port, you can see St Peter's tower, a 20-metre tall cylindrical tower constructed during the Hellenistic period. This is one of the best preserved towers in the Cyclades, and was used to defend the surrounding area.

Gavrio Port

The small port town is the first thing you will see in Andros. It's less lively that you might expect, probably due to the fact that Batsi makes up for it. There are a few tavernas, cafes, bakeries and rooms, though it wouldn't be our first choice of places to stay in Andros. You can find several rent-a-car and other tourist services, as well as a big pharmacy which seems to be open at most times.

Korthi Town

Korthi (Korthio / Korthion) is a sleepy little town to the south of the island that's worth stopping at for a coffee and a chat with the locals. Just pick any of the cafes and tavernas on the picturesque promenade, with lovely views down to the sea. The town itself has some very picturesque houses, and the local beaches Korthi and Vintsi are fairly well protected from the winds. In fact, Korthi beach was one of our favourite beaches on a windy day.

Menites Village

Situated halfway inland between Chora and the west coast, Menites is a small village with several water fountains. If you didn't know you were in Andros, you would probably imagine you are somewhere in North Greece – it is an unusually lush place for a Cycladic island. There are a few cafes and tavernas here. If you want to experience more of the beautiful nature, a hiking path goes straight through the village.

Apikia Village

This small, picturesque village just a short drive from Chora is popular for the famous Sariza springs and the nearby factory where the local water is bottled. The water is said to be therapeutic for people suffering from kidney issues. If you visit in the evening, you may want to bring a jacket!

Stenies Village

Right next door to Apikia, Stenies is considered by many to be one of the most beautiful villages in Andros. There's a free parking lot just outside the town where you can leave your vehicle, and then take a wander around. You will discover the typical white-washed Cycladic houses, and several churches and chapels - ask the locals, as there are more than 25 in this small village!

If you are in Andros for Greek Easter, you should definitely head to Stenies for Easter Sunday. One of the local customs involves the firing of hundreds of purpose-made cannons called maskoula and releasing fireworks. It's worth observing, though if you are visiting with small children you may want to think about it - there will be a lot of explosions and smoke!

Paleopolis Ancient Town

Paleopolis on the west coast, to the south of Batsi, was the capital of Andros between 6th century BC and 6th century AD, when the first Arab invasions happened. Remains of the ancient town can be seen on the island, whereas the findings that have been excavated are presented in the small archaeological museum.

If you are interested in hiking, you can walk down to the coast, preferably on a non-windy day. You can still see some of the fortifications of the town, while the remains of the ancient port are visible under the sea.

Faneromenis Castle

The Faneromenis Castle is located up on the mountain, close to Kochylos village. It was built in the beginning of the

13th century by the same Venetian ruler who built the castle in Chora. You can still see what's left of the walls, as well as the adjacent Faneromeni church, celebrating on the 15th August. As you would expect, the views from the castle are pretty unique.

Aladinou Cave

On your way from Batsi to Chora, you will see a few signs for Aladinou Cave, also known as Foros Cave. This is a small cave with stalactites and stalagmites, estimated to be over 4.5 million years old.

You can have a short guided tour by some very enthusiastic locals, who will show you some stalagmites in the making! It's well worth visiting, and easy to fit in on a road trip around the island.

12. Museums in Andros

Among Greeks, Andros has a reputation as an island with an important naval and cultural tradition. Several wealthy benefactors have lived here, and they have left a rich legacy in the form of donations, foundations, and plenty of museums.

Most of the museums in Andros are located in Chora, but there are also a few more scattered around the island. Opening times tend to vary between seasons, and online information is often scarce, outdated or just in Greek, so it might be best to confirm by a quick call.

Goulandris Museum of Contemporary Art, Chora

This private museum was originally established by the Goulandris family in order to host the works of an Andriot sculptor, Michael Tombros, who also created the Unknown Sailor's statue. The museum was later expanded, and today consists of two buildings.

While the Old Wing is home to artworks of prominent Greek artists, the New Wing hosts temporary exhibitions, presenting works of Greek and foreign painters. You may be surprised to hear that works of artists like Picasso, Matisse, Miro and Kandinsky have been exhibited here.

Opening times vary by season, so check their fully functional website for more information.

https://goulandris.gr/en/
E-mail: info@goulandris.gr
Tel: 22820-22444

Archaeological Museum of Andros, Chora

The Archaeological Museum of Andros is a small museum exhibiting several collections of items from the Geometric, Archaic, Roman, pre-Byzantine and Byzantine periods. Although it isn't the most exciting archaeological museum in the world, there are a few sculptures and inscriptions worth seeing if you are visiting Andros.

Summer opening times: Wed, Fri - Mon 8:30 - 16:00. Closed on Tuesdays and Thursdays.
Tel: 22820-23664.

Maritime Museum of Andros, Chora

The Maritime Museum showcases the rich naval tradition of Andros. It contains several maritime and nautical documents, such as diaries and contracts, as well as ship models, photos, lithographs etc. It is located towards the edge of the town, close to the square with the Unknown Sailor's statue.

Information regarding their opening times was conflicting at the time of research. You could try visiting between 11.00-14.00 and 18.00-21.00 daily, excluding Wednesdays. Alternatively, call 22820-22264.

Petros and Marika Kydonieos Foundation, Chora

Another private initiative, the Kydonieos Foundation aims to promote exhibitions and cultural events in Andros. The Foundation provides several all-year-round workshops, including instrument lessons, pottery classes etc. Furthermore, it organizes rotating art exhibitions in summer, featuring prominent Greek artists.

The building is located towards the entrance of the Chora. When exhibitions are on, their summer opening times are normally Mon, Wed - Sat 10.00-13.30 and 18.30 - 21.30, and Sun 10.00 -14.00. Closed on Tuesdays.

For confirmation or any other information, you can call 22820-24598.

Kairios Library, Chora

This library is home to a large collection of documents, publications, manuscripts and several other Andros archives.

Unless you can speak Greek this might not be very interesting, although fans of architecture will appreciate the unique building interior.

According to their website (in Greek only), they should be open 9.00-13.00 on weekdays. You can e-mail them at kaireios@otenet.gr or try calling on 22820-22262.

Digital Museum of Andros, Chora

This is a museum projecting digital content about the history of Andros. It's probably the best museum in Chora Andros if you are visiting with family!

For summer, the museum is open 11.00-14.00 and 18.00-21.00 daily, excluding Wednesdays. That said, there is very little online information, so you could try reaching them on 22820-24720 to confirm.

Folklore and Christian Art Museum, Chora

If you are interested in traditional local life and Christian artefacts, you can visit this small museum which is inside the Paradise Hotel in Chora. At the time of research, it was open on weekends in July and throughout August, but it might be best to call and confirm at 22820-22187.

Olive Oil Museum, Ano Pitrofos

One really interesting museum in Andros is the Olive Oil Museum in Ano Pitrofos. Even if you have been to an olive oil museum before, you should make a special trip to Ano Pitrofos just to visit this one.

The museum is located in an old, authentic olive mill, and the founder, Dimitris Chelmis, is a passionate architect who restored the mill transforming it into a museum. Projects like these bridge the gap between the past and present, helping to keep traditions alive. They need all the support they can get, so definitely pay a visit!

You will have a short guided tour, followed by a video Dimitris made after the mill was restored, showing how olive oil is produced. This is a great museum to bring young kids, as they will love playing with the old equipment.

http://www.musioelias.gr/en/node/25
E-mail: info@musioelias.gr
Tel 6932-731776

Archaeological Museum of Paleopolis

This small museum is located close to Batsi, on the way to Chora. It contains findings from the excavations of Paleopolis, which was the capital of the island in ancient times. Summer opening times: Wed - Mon 8:30 - 16:00. Closed on Tuesdays. Tel 22820-41985

13. Monasteries in Andros

Like most of Greece, Andros has many monasteries. Some of them date from the Byzantine period, while others are newer. Even if you are not particularly interested in the Greek Orthodox religion, you could visit one or two and get an idea of life in a monastery.

Zoodochos Pigi Monastery

The largest monastery in Andros, Zoodochos Pigi is an easy one to stop by, as it's located close to Batsi and Gavrio. It may have been established as early as the 9th century AD, initially as a male monastery. It changed to a women's monastery in 1928.

The monastery's museum contains religious artworks, icons and rare books and manuscripts, as well as some prehistoric tools found in the area. If you happen to be in Andros for Easter, try to visit the monastery on the first Friday after Easter Sunday, when there are interesting traditional celebrations.

Agios Nikolaos Monastery

The impressive Agios Nikolaos monastery, close to Apikia village, was probably established in the 11th century, though the existing construction was raised later. During the time of the Ottoman Empire it served as a place of resistance and a secret underground school, like many other monasteries in Greece.

Exhibits in the monastery include icons, artworks and sacred relics. You can reach the monastery through narrow dirt roads from either Vourkoti or Apikia villages.

Panachrantou Monastery

If you are feeling a little more adventurous, you can visit Panachrantou Monastery, up on the mountains. The road to Panachrantou Monastery is narrow and winding – but that's part of the fun of getting there!

This old Byzantine monastery dates from the 9th century AD, and is home to an icon of the Virgin Mary and the relics of St. Panteleimon. Most of it has been refurbished however, and it somehow feels brand new. Still, it's definitely worth visiting, if only for the wonderful views. If you are visiting Andros in spring, do not miss the Easter celebrations here. You can get in touch on 22820-51090.

Agia Eirini Monastery

Founded in 1780 as a male monastery, Agia Eirini monastery later functioned as a nunnery and was abandoned in 1833. It was refurbished to high standards due to private initiative, and nowadays operates as a children's summer school camp.

Visitors can explore the various collections that operate in the monastery, such as the collection of traditional musical instruments and a private collection of fossils, minerals and rocks. Opening times are 10.00-18.00 daily.

You can reach them on imagiaseirinisandrou@gmail.com or 6982-038281.

14. Beaches in Andros

For many Greeks, some of the main attractions in Andros are its lovely beaches. Even if you spend a week in Andros, you could easily visit a few different beaches every day and still run out of time to explore all of them.

According to locals, Andros has over 170 beaches, many of which are easily accessible by car. Others are a little more difficult to get to, as they require a drive on a dirt road, a hike or even a boat trip.

Batsi Beach

If you are staying in Batsi, this is an easy option for a quick swim. You will find many umbrellas and loungers, but there are also more quiet areas where you can put your towel.

Kypri, Chrissi Ammos and Agios Petros Beaches

These three sandy beaches are located between Batsi and Gavrio port. They are all fairly large, easily accessible, and offer several options in terms of umbrellas, loungers and tavernas.

These beaches are probably your best bet if you don't have a car, as you can easily get there by bus and you will always find a nice spot to stop at. They are also ideal for families, as they are relatively shallow and protected. Windsurfing and other beachsports facilities are also available.

Fellos and Kourtali Beaches

These are two of our favourite beaches in Andros, located on the north west of the island, just past Gavrio. They are two long, sandy beaches that are very close to each other, and can be fairly protected from the Meltemi even on a very windy day.

Bring your own shade, water and snacks, and enjoy. On your way back, you can stop at To Steki tou Andrea for a nice meal – the cheese selection and the lamb dishes are great!

Vlychada and Pyrgos Beaches

If you like quiet beaches and are prepared for a 15-minute drive on a narrow dirt road, Vlychada might be your favourite beach in Andros. In September, you might even have the entire beach for yourself.

The nearby Pyrgos is a lot smaller, but a little more protected from the wind. You can spend all day here if you like.

On the way back, make sure you go to the taverna O Kossis, which we thought was the best restaurant in Andros – more on that later on.

Grias To Pidima Beach

The most famous beach in Andros is "Grias To Pidima", roughly translated as "the Old Lady's Jump". You may have seen the photo of a tall, thin stone pillar coming out of the sea.

According to one story, the pillar is actually an old lady that jumped from the Faneromenis Castle, above the beach, to escape from the Ottomans. True enough – if you look closely at the stone, you may see that it resembles a woman from some angles.

While this beach is very picturesque, it gets quite busy, and is best avoided on days of strong Meltemi wind as it's not very protected.

Try to get there early in the day, and bring your own water and a few snacks. You will have to walk down some stairs in order to get to the beach.

Korthi and Vintsi Beaches

A long, surprisingly quiet sandy beach, Korthi beach is a great choice, and you can even get some natural shade. It's also a good alternative if Grias to Pidima beach is too windy or too busy.

There is a smaller cove at the other side of Korthi town called Vintsi, where the locals prefer to swim.

Paraporti and Niborio Beaches

If you are staying at Chora, the easiest beach to go to is Paraporti, known also as Paraportiani, just a short walk from the town. It's a fairly popular beach, even on windy days.

Niborio or Neimporio, on the other side of the town, is rather pebbly and we wouldn't suggest it on a windy day as the waves can get dangerous.

Gialia and Piso Gialia Beaches

These two bays are a short drive from Chora and Stenies, and Piso Gialia is the nicer of the two. To get there, you will need to walk down a fair few stairs.

There is a rather loud beach bar, though it shouldn't matter as there is a lot of free space on the beach where you can put your towel.

Apothikes Beach

This small beach on the west of the island came highly recommended by locals. You can get there through a very steep dirt road. The beach has a bar, but you can bring your own food and drinks if you prefer.

Zorkos, Vitali, Ateni and Achla Beaches

These remote sandy beaches are among the best in Andros. They are accessible through long dirt roads, so if you want to rent a car in Andros consider getting a 4WD.

It is also possible to hike there, or perhaps take a boat trip, depending on the weather. As they are facing north, they are not recommended in case of Meltemi winds, because they will be very affected.

15. Outdoor Activities in Andros

Whether you're feeling adventurous or simply want a stroll in the great outdoors, there's plenty of outdoor activities to choose from in Andros.

Hiking in Andros

Andros is a very enjoyable place to go hiking. The mountainous, green island has a very long network of hiking trails and paths, of which at least 150 kms have been cleared, maintained and signposted in recent years. Works were undertaken by the Cyclades Prefecture and also several groups of volunteers, such as Andros Routes.
https://www.androsroutes.gr/

The hiking trails of Andros received the "Leading Quality Trails – Best of Europe" Award in 2015. Additionally, the "Andros Foot Festival" is organized annually in October, promoting hiking tourism on the island.

https://www.androsonfootfestival.gr/en/

One of the most unique features of Andros, and what makes hiking there so special, is its diverse landscapes. Andros is mountainous and rugged, but also has many springs and waterfalls, which is quite rare for a Cycladic island.

While hiking around Andros, you can see several man-made structures, like bridges, olive presses and numerous churches and chapels. You can also visit some of the caves, such as Aladinou or Vitali.

There are several networks and companies offering hiking activities in Andros, and you can also choose to go on your own – just make sure you have good shoes and preferably a local map.

Some of the most popular routes include the hike from Vourkoti to Achla beach, the hike to Pithara waterfalls, the trail to Panachrantou Monastery and the route around Menites.

Best Time: You might find hiking in Andros a little challenging in summer, as the weather will be hot. Spring and autumn are the best seasons to go hiking in Andros.

Watersports and Diving in Andros

We can't stress it enough - for people who love beaches, Andros is a true paradise. There are dozens of gorgeous beaches, and you won't have time to see them all in a week. The locals will tell you that the island has over 170 beaches. The coastline is a whopping 176 kms, so we absolutely believe them!

Apart from topping up your tan on the beach, there are many sea-related activities in Andros. If you want to explore underwater Greece, you can go snorkeling or scuba diving. Consult ScubAndros at Gavrio port whether you are after a fun dive, a PADI license, or a snorkeling trip. https://scuba-andros.gr/

If you are an experienced diver, there are many wonderful spots where you can dive in Andros. Greece may not have the colourful fish of SE Asia, but there are many fascinating shipwrecks. You can also go diving around Paleopoli, and discover parts of the submerged ancient city.

Not a fan of being underwater? No worries. You can try watersports such as surfing, windsurf or SUP. WeSurfin, based on Kypri beach, are a team with impressive bios, and are experts in these sports. They also provide fun water games, whether you are travelling with children or with your friends. http://www.wesurfin.com/en/

Keep Safe: Andros can get very windy, especially during the Meltemi season, which is normally July and August. Your safety is first! If you are swimming, snorkeling or windsurfing on your own, make sure you take all necessary precautions. Always stay close to the coast, as the currents are deceptively strong – you don't want to end up in Tinos!

16. Eating in Andros

While Andros is an island, pretty much every local we met advised us to avoid eating fish! We found that rather surprising, but decided to follow their advice and try some of the local meat dishes instead. The meat is either grilled, or cooked in different sauces.

A popular dish, normally cooked over Easter, is a whole lamb or goat stuffed with cheese, eggs and herbs, called *lambriatis*.

Additionally, Andros has several local cheeses, made from cow, goat and sheep milk. They are all delicious, and you can either get them at restaurants or at small local markets and supermarkets. Our favourite was fresh *volaki* cheese, which is shaped in the form of little balls. *Kopanisti*, a spicy creamy cheese, and *petroti*, another fresh white cheese, are also very tasty.

In terms of other local dishes, there are special omelettes in Andros, called *fourtalia* or *froutalia*. They contain thinly sliced potatoes, sausages and maybe *louza*, pieces of pork which have been smoked and marinated in wine. Some people also add vegetables, or cheese.

Finally, Andros also has many traditional desserts, such as spoon sweets and marzipan cakes called *amygdalota*. We somehow didn't try any of those when we were there. It's as good an excuse as any for wanting to return to Andros!

In terms of restaurants, there are many great places to eat in Andros, with an average budget per person at around 15 euro, based on two sharing. Cards are widely accepted, though no-one will complain if you want to pay cash.

O Kossis restaurant, near Kato Fellos

Our favourite taverna in Andros was a meat taverna called O Kossis (Kosses on Google Maps). It's up on the mountain in the middle of nowhere to the north of the island, so you will need your own transportation to get there. It's about a half hour's drive from Batsi, and it's absolutely worth it.

They specialize in grilled meat, and they are really experts, which explains the number of customers they get. If you are a vegetarian, go for a freshly made salad with local vegetables and cheese and some of the best fries we've ever had. There's also a farm with a small area where they give pony rides. If you are travelling with family, your children will love it!

The bill comes with a lovely treat - home-made *raki* and yoghurt with dessert. Yum!

Mi se meli, Batsi

If you are staying in Batsi, you can try this more modern restaurant in a narrow alleyway, which came highly recommended. Do not miss the fava beans with truffle oil, a totally unexpected but fantastic combination.

O Stamatis, Batsi

A no-frills local taverna with many traditional dishes, o Stamatis is a busy place with a standard tourist menu and hearty portions. The food was nice and fairly priced.

To Steki tou Andrea, Fellos

This was one of our favourite tavernas in Andros. We had some of the special dishes, including a selection of local homemade cheeses that were the best we had on the island. The taverna is fairly popular, so it may be best to reserve a table if you are going at busy times of the day.

To Balkoni tou Aigaiou, Ano Aprovato

People go to this great taverna close to Batsi for great food and sunset views. Make sure to bring a jacket!

Giannoulis, Agios Petros

Traditional home-made food, such as rooster in wine sauce and aubergines in the oven. If they have the *karydopita* walnut cake, try it.

Endochora, Chora

This is a great place for modern Mediterranean cuisine with interesting starters and green salads. They also serve a special ice cream called *soumada*.

Nonas, Chora

A fish and seafood taverna on Niborio beach, serving fish that are caught daily by the family. Make sure you reserve a table as it's popular with locals!

17. Nightlife in Andros

If you are looking for a Mykonos style party scene, Andros is not exactly the place to be. While you can find some bars and nightlife, don't go to Andros expecting late nights and lots of hard clubbing. At the same time, the island is full of all-day beach bars where you can have snacks, coffee and drinks pretty much all day long.

Regardless, if you are looking for some nightlife, most of the options on the island are in Batsi and Chora. **Capriccio** is probably people's favourite option in Batsi, along with **Buka bar**, but just walk around and see if there is another one you like more. As for Chora, **Levels** and **Lithi** are some of the best places for a nice, relaxing drink.

Note that the drive from Batsi to Chora takes around an hour, and it's a winding mountain road with no lights. Therefore, if you are staying in Andros for several days and want to experience the nightlife, you might want to base yourself in both places, for a few days each.

18. Tinos Island Travel Guide - Map

Turn your book to the side to read the map!

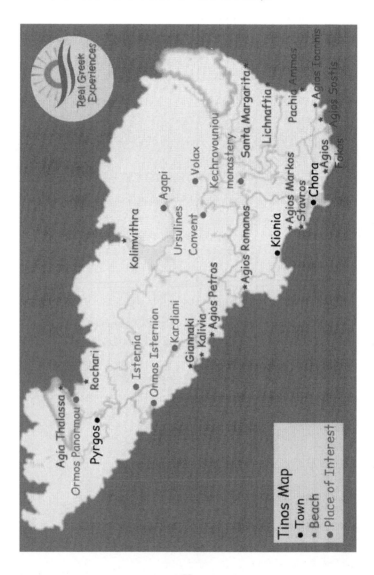

19. Introduction to Tinos Island

Location: Cyclades Island Group
Population: 8,600 (approx)
Capital: Tinos Town / Chora (Τήνος / Χώρα)
Ferry Port: Chora
Hospital: Tinos Health Centre, Mark. Krikeli 18, Chora, Tel 22833-60000
Police: Chora, 22830-22100

Tinos is another one of the 26 inhabited islands in the Cyclades island group in Greece. Although Tinos and Andros appear almost within touching distance on a map, they are about 2 hours away from each other by ferry because of the locations of the ports. Other islands close to Tinos are Delos and Mykonos.

With a permanent population of nearly 9,000 people, and an area of 197 square kilometres, the island is active all year around, unlike smaller islands which virtually shut down in the winter months. It's something of a religious center, and if you ask most Greeks about Tinos, they will immediately associate it with the Church of Panagia Evangelistria and the pilgrimages people take there.

There is, however, much more to Tinos than just its very famous church. To begin with, there are the stunningly unique dovecotes (pigeon houses), scattered all around the island. Tinos has some amazing beaches, over 50 villages each with their own distinctive character, windmills, hiking paths, Venetian fortifications and so much more! Tinos has been compared to Mykonos as "twice as nice at half the price", and who are we to argue?

This guide will show you where to stay and places to visit in Tinos. Whether you spend just a couple of days on the island, or stay for a week, there's plenty to do!

Don't Leave Tinos Without Seeing

- Church of Panagia Evangelistria in Chora
- Volax village and the boulders
- Pyrgos village and the museums
- Kardiani village
- Isternia village
- The dovecotes all around the island

20. Where to Stay in Tinos

If you haven't been to Tinos before, you will probably be overwhelmed when it comes to accommodation. There are several beautiful villages and resort towns to choose from. Our guide on where to stay in Tinos will help you narrow down your choices.

Depending on how you are planning to get around Tinos, and on what you want to get out of your holiday, you can either stay at one of the beach resorts, a mountain village, or even in Chora. There are a wide selection of apartments and small hotels to suit all travelers.

For a full guide on where to stay in Tinos along with an interactive map, visit:

Hotels in Agios Ioannis Porto

Agios Ioannis Porto is located at the southeast part of the island. It is a quiet settlement with a range of rooms and apartments to let, a few restaurants and a selection of nice sandy beaches nearby.

There is a fairly frequent bus to Chora, but if you decide to stay in Agios Ioannis Porto and want to be flexible in terms of moving around, you will be better off renting a car. Driving here from Chora takes about 10 minutes.

We stayed at **Studios Kyklades**, offering modern, clean apartments with spacious bedrooms and fully equipped kitchens with everything you may need. There's a view of the crescent bay nearby, and good parking for vehicles. It was great for a couple, but would also be comfortable for a family of up to four people.

Hotels in Agios Sostis

Close to Agios Ioannis Porto, you can find another beach resort, Agios Sostis, with plenty of accommodation to choose from. You can reach Agios Sostis by the same bus that goes from Chora to Agios Ioannis Porto. Note that some of the buses do not take you to Agios Sostis beach, but it's just a short walk from the bus stop.

One of the best places to stay in Agios Sostis is **Summer Time – Tinos apartments**, offering newly built accommodation with kitchenettes and an on-site snack bar.

Hotels in Chora Tinos

The Chora in Tinos isn't nearly as picturesque as the main towns on other Cycladic islands – it's a rather built up town dominated by the big Panagia Evangelistria church and an array of souvenir shops. However, it's a good choice for people who are after a little bit of nightlife – though don't expect tons of clubbing and partying.

Note that some of the roads in Chora are closed to traffic in summer evenings. If you have your own vehicle, make sure you know the traffic rules.

Chora has a wide selection of places to stay. **Vincenzo Family Rooms**, right in the centre of the town, is one of the best choices. They have suites, rooms and apartments, and also offer spa facilities!

If you want to be close to the town but still in a quiet location, you can check out the more luxurious **Santamare Villa and Apartments** close to Agios Fokas beach. They also have a pool, ideal for those windy days.

Hotels in Kionia

Kionia is probably your best bet if you are looking for a cosmopolitan beach – by Tinian standards. This seemed to be the most lively area in terms of beachfront hotels and tavernas, but still has plenty of space on the beach. As it is fairly open to the strong northern winds, you can go swimming at the nearby coves of Agios Markos and Stavros, on the way to Chora, which are a lot more protected.

There are several buses a day from Kionia to Chora and back. If you have a car, it takes around 5 minutes to drive – you could even walk there if you wanted.

One of the best choices of accommodation in Kionia is **Didymes Studios**, offering beautifully decorated studios and apartments with kitchenettes, in a lovely garden setting.

Hotels in Agios Romanos

This is a small, self-contained resort area with a few places to stay, a couple of beach bars and a handful of tavernas. The bay seems fairly protected from the Meltemi winds, compared to other places on the island.

You can get there through some winding mountain roads, and some people might prefer to avoid driving at night. Sunsets, on the other hand, are spectacular! At the time of writing there is no bus there, so it's best to stay here if you have your own transportation.

Self-catering **En Plo Apartments** offer a range of options at reasonable prices in Agios Romanos - and the views couldn't be any better!

Hotels in Pyrgos

If you don't care much about being right on the coast, you could consider staying in the picturesque mountain village of Pyrgos, to the north of the island. Pyrgos is a popular half day trip for people who visit Tinos, and you will see visitors arriving from Chora on organised buses and coaches. Confusingly, Google Maps shows this village as Panormos!

Pyrgos is a fairly large village, full of pretty white-washed houses and narrow alleys. There are plenty of beautiful marble artworks and the quaint Pyrgos cemetery, courtesy of the famous Tinian sculptors. Visit the local museums, to learn more about them.

Pyrgos is a great base if you have your own transportation, as there are very few buses a day to Chora and back. It is also the ideal area to stay if you want to explore the northern beaches that are close by, Agia Thalassa, Ormos Panormou and Rochari.

In terms of accommodation, *Villa Celeste* is a fantastic place to stay, and can accommodate up to 12 guests. Located in a beautiful, quiet spot, it has a swimming pool for those windy Meltemi days.

Hotels near Volax

One of our favourite villages in Tinos was Volax. It's a really small village in a fascinating area full of huge, rounded granite stones. While the village itself doesn't have too much to do, it is very pretty, and it would be great to meet some locals and know more about life in the area.

Staying close to Volax would also make sense for anyone who wants to go hiking, climbing or bouldering in the nearby area - more on this later.

White Tinos Luxury Suites in nearby Steni, Exomvourgo, is an ideal choice. Guests comment on how clean and friendly it is, and especially like the breakfasts!

There are hundreds of other places to stay in Tinos. For an interactive map and easy way to book hotels online, visit: https://www.davestravelpages.com/tinos-hotels-where-to-stay-in-tinos/

21. How to Get Around Tinos

Tinos is a very special island. While there are many beautiful beaches, the real attractions of Tinos in Greece are its picturesque villages, hundreds of churches, the strange dovecotes, and the unique landscapes. But how do you get to see it all?

This chapter is designed to help you get around Tinos, and includes advice for driving in Tinos, as well as public transport options.

Getting around Tinos by Car

Getting around Tinos by car is the best way if you want to be independent. It might take you a bit of time to get used to the local roads, but as soon as you do you will enjoy it a lot.

Rent a Car in Tinos

There are maybe half a dozen, if not more, Tinos car hire services around the port area, so there's plenty of places to choose from. A quick Google of car hire companies in Tinos will give you a good starting point of places to go to. Vidalis, Dimitris and Avance are all fairly popular choices.

Prices depend on the season and the model, and you can always bargain, especially if you are visiting during the off-season and booking the car on the spot. American visitors who may not be used to 'driving stick' will need to see if any automatic cars are available. An International Driving License is required for many nationalities, so make sure you have this before you travel to Greece.

Driving around Tinos

Driving around Tinos is great fun. That said, you will need to get used to no traffic lights, narrow roads, uneven surfaces and lots of dirt roads! A regular car will be fine for most of the places you will want to get to, and it's actually better to have a small car as it will be easier to find parking spots outside the villages.

Most of the roads in Tinos are sealed and in pretty good condition, but there are also long stretches of dirt roads. If you want to explore the whole of the island, it might be best to rent a 4WD. If hiring a car, check what your insurance covers you for in terms of road types.

Some additional notes for driving in Tinos: Google maps works fine everywhere. In terms of parking, you will typically have to park at designated areas outside the villages. Also, note that access to some areas in Tinos town is restricted between 20.45 and midnight, at least in summer.

Getting around Tinos by ATV or Motorbike

As well as car hire, motorbike and ATV rental is also available, although not as popular as might be expected.

Perhaps this is to do with the strong winds in July and August, where riding one would be either difficult or unpleasant.

Unlike other parts of the world, you will need a valid driver's license if you want to rent any of these in Greece. You will spot several companies close to the port, so if you haven't pre-booked you can choose on the spot.

Getting around Tinos by Bus

If you have been to Greece before, you will know that each area has its own local bus service, called the KTEL. Tinos is no exception, and in fact the local bus service is quite frequent, compared to some other islands.

People planning to get around Tinos by bus might be better off staying in either Chora (generally referred to as Tinos) or Kionia town by the beach. If you choose to stay in Agios Ioannis Porto / Agios Sostis and want to see other parts of the island by bus, you would need to take a bus into Chora first, and then swap to another service.

Various local buses go to most of the interesting villages and beaches around Tinos. In theory, it would be possible to see most of the villages on buses. In practice this would take you several days, as there are well over 30 villages worth stopping at and the buses only run a few times per day.

If you only want to see 3-4 villages and spend the rest of your time by the beach, you can comfortably get around Tinos by bus.

Note that there are no buses running late in the evening, so if you want to explore the villages at night you will have to use some other form of transportation.

Getting around Tinos by Taxi

If you prefer to use taxis and private transfers in Tinos, it's definitely possible. Asteras is a taxi service that can be contacted on 22830-26000, 6936-561676 and 6974-926410.

Alternatively, you can get in touch with Tinos luxury taxi services, offering transportation services and tours of the island. http://www.tinosprivatetaxi.gr/

Getting around Tinos by Bicycle

For people who are up for a challenge, Tinos would be a great place to cycle. Avoid summer, and you should be off to a rewarding experience, but don't expect easy rides, especially if you want to see many of the villages.

Although Tinos is less mountainous than nearby Andros, it is probably not for beginners. If you are planning a cycling trip to the Greek islands, it's best to schedule it in spring or autumn.

Getting around Tinos on Foot

If you are into hiking, Tinos is a great destination. There are many hiking paths and trails all around the island, and they are very well signposted. We walked along a few parts of the main hiking trails and it was really enjoyable.

People planning to hike in Tinos will really only need good footwear. It's best to avoid summer and plan your trip for spring or autumn instead. One of the nicest trails seems to be the one leading from Volax to Agapi village, both of which are favourites with visitors to the island.

Getting around Tinos by Boat

Depending on how strong the Meltemi wind is, you can explore Tinos and the nearby islands by sea. Here's your chance to visit Delos, which is otherwise only accessible through Mykonos. You can find more information on https://www.tinosseatours.com/

Final Thoughts

While renting a car offers more flexibility, driving on the Greek islands is not for everyone. The bus network is pretty good, so if you only want to visit a few places in Tinos, you can easily do it just on buses. For those who prefer to explore more of the island, a car is a better option.

See if driving in Greece is your thing in this article https://realgreekexperiences.com/driving-in-greece-essential-tips-on-greek-driving-from-a-local

22. Villages and Places of Interest in Tinos

For most non-religious visitors, the main attractions of Tinos are its quaint villages. It's just about possible to see the most important villages in Tinos in a couple of days, if you start early and make the most of your time. You would need several days to explore them all.

Chora Tinos

The main settlement in Tinos is referred to as Chora, Tinos, or sometimes Poli, from the Greek word for "town". Located on the south-west of the island, this is also the island's port.

In all honesty, it's not the most picturesque town in the Cyclades islands as it's pretty built up. This means the awe factor of seeing many of the white-and-blue houses that are so representative of this area of Greece is absent.

Making up for this though, is the main focal point for many visitors to the island - the Panagia Evangelistria church.

Panagia Evangelistria Church in Chora Tinos

By Greek standards, this is a very big church, and it's one of the most important Greek Orthodox churches in the country. It is open on a daily basis from early in the morning until late in the evening, though it appears busier in the mornings, when visitors come for a pilgrimage.

A Nun with a Vision

The story of how the Panagia Evangelistria church was built is quite interesting.

Shortly after Greece had been liberated from the Ottoman Empire, a Greek Orthodox nun, Agia Pelagia, had a vision. In that vision, the Virgin Mary explained where to find the Icon of Her Annunciation, which was buried in the ground. After the Icon was discovered, the Church of Panagia Evangelistria was built at the site.

There are two main streets going down from the church, where you can buy souvenirs, mostly leaning on the religious side. As for the red carpet stretching all the way from the port to the church, it is meant for people visiting

Tinos on a pilgrimage, who will typically head to the church on their knees and hands.

Chora Tinos during Greek Easter

If you happen to be in Tinos for Greek Easter, do not miss the midnight ceremony on Good Saturday, when the Resurrection happens. Hundreds of people gather outside the church, expecting the Holy Light from Jerusalem.

You can then enjoy a traditional meal of *mayiritsa*, a hearty soup containing liver, other obscure and possibly less savory but very tasty animal parts and a thick lemon-and-egg sauce.

Here's a little more about Greek Easter traditions
https://realgreekexperiences.com/greek-easter-traditions

Similarly, on the 15th of August, the Assumption Day is celebrated, with thousands of people visiting to pay their respects.

The Museums around the Panagia Evangelistria Church

Around the church's spacious courtyard, you will find a series of rooms that host several exhibitions of artworks and religious objects.

Namely, you can visit the Portrait Gallery, the Ecclesiastical Heirloom and Icon Exhibition, the Ambry, the Museum of Anthony Sohos and the Museum of Tinian artists upstairs.

All these collections are free to visit, though photography is not allowed.

Even if you are not religious you will definitely enjoy the various Byzantine icons, some of which are hundreds of years old. You will also get a chance to see some works by famous Greek artists.

A special space inside the church's courtyard is reserved for Elli's Mausoleum, dedicated to the first victims of WWII in Greece. They were killed when an Italian torpedo hit the Greek warship Elli, on 15th August 1940.

Archaeological Museum in Chora Tinos

Apart from the church, you can also visit the small Archaeological Museum in Tinos. It's a relatively small museum, and perhaps a little underwhelming. It won't take you more than a half hour to see the exhibits.

Pyrgos Village

If you only have time for one village in Tinos, make sure you go to Pyrgos. It is a large, picturesque village up on the mountain in the north-west of the island, and is often included in half-day bus tours from Chora. Note that if you are driving around Tinos and using Google Maps, Pyrgos is confusingly shown as Panormos.

Pyrgos is very well kept, and you will really enjoy walking around. For us, its main attractions were its museums, the marble works and the atmospheric cemetery.

If you are going around Tinos by car, it's best to leave it in the designated parking area just before you get into the village. Then you can easily explore Pyrgos on foot, as everything is in walking distance.

There are three great museums in Pyrgos – the Museum of Marble Crafts, the Tinian Artists Museum and the Giannoulis Halepas Museum. It doesn't really matter what order you visit them in.

The Museum of Marble Crafts

The Museum of Marble Crafts explains everything you wanted to know about marble and the art of sculpting. While at first this may not sound too exciting, it was actually very interesting to visit and really well put together.

There are videos showing the procedures that the marble goes through, from being quarried to being transformed into beautiful artwork. It made us appreciate every single church we later saw in Tinos, let alone the ancient Greek statues!

Here, you can also familiarize yourselves with the names and the works of the most prominent Tinian artists.

In summer months, the museum is open daily (except Tuesdays) from 10.00-18.00. Check their website for more information. https://www.piop.gr/

The Tinian Artists Museum

The Tinian Artists Museum is a small museum showcasing some of the works of famous Tinian artists. Although it might be more relevant for Greek people, it was still interesting to see a selection of sculptures and hear some stories about the artists. If you have already been to the museum of Marble Crafts, you might be able to recognize some of the artists' names.

The Museum of Giannoulis Halepas

The Museum of Giannoulis Halepas is the original house of one of the most prominent Greek sculptors, Giannoulis Halepas. His story is truly a very sad one. As he was very attached to his art, he was pretty much confined by his family, who thought he was mad. After his mother's death, he was free to create several magnificent works, many of which are very famous all around Greece.

The last two museums have a joint ticket, and in summer they were open all day long. Opening times may depend upon the season though, and change from year to year. You can get in touch at 22830-22256 to confirm their opening times.

Pyrgos Cemetery

Do not leave Pyrgos without visiting the quaint cemetery, which is decorated with fascinating marble works by several sculptors. Try to find a Greek speaking person to translate some of the plaques for you.

Pyrgos during Greek Easter

If you happen to be in Tinos for Greek Easter, it's worth taking a special trip to observe the magnificent Epitafios procession on Good Friday. This is a particularly solemn religious ceremony, representing the saddest event for Orthodox Christians, the death of Jesus Christ.

During the procession, a flower-laden construction called the Epitafios is taken around the village. The Epitafios is really a replica of the coffin of Jesus Christ. People follow the procession carrying lit candles and the event is truly memorable for visitors.

Pyrgos is also worth visiting on Easter Sunday, when the Easter festivities take place. The dish of the day is the famous lamb on the spit, accompanied by red eggs!

Isternia Village

Isternia (or Ysternia) village is just a short drive from Pyrgos, and is one of the largest and most important villages in Tinos. Many of the famous Tinian sculptors were born here. There is a small museum of Isternian artists, exhibiting their works. Apart from that, there are many impressive marble works to see all around the village, most notably the churches of Holy Trinity and Agia Paraskevi. Close to Isternia, you will see a group of old windmills and two little churches.

Kardiani Village

passed too steep

A short drive to the south further on from Isternia, is Kardiani - a lovely village built right on a slope. You can leave your car at the designated parking area, and walk around the stairs and uneven little streets.

The village has the traditional white-and-blue houses that you would expect to see in a Cycladic island, and is really very picturesque. You may not notice it immediately, but there are both an Orthodox and a Catholic church in Kardiani.

On Easter Monday, Kardiani hosts a fantastic local celebration with music and traditional food, so keep that in mind if you are in Tinos for Greek Easter.

Volax Village

This is another quaint village in Tinos, pretty much at the centre of the south part of the island. The wider area surrounding the village is also called Volax, and is fascinating, as it's full of massive round granite stones. The landscape is really cool, and you are only likely to meet a few cows and goats, and maybe the odd tourist.

If you decide to rent a 4WD, follow the dirt roads towards the wider area of Falatados, up on the mountain, and then get back to Volax. You can also do this in a regular car, but check with your car rental company that it will be ok to do so first.

What are these Boulders around Volax Village?

There are different theories as to how these stones got there.

Was it the result of a volcanic explosion, over 20 million years ago? Could it be that the rocks were under the sea, and were rounded off because of the sea water and the sand? Are they just a common natural phenomenon, where granite is gradually rounded off because of the winds and chemical reactions? Perhaps it was the Titans who threw those stones over Tinos?

Who knows – all we can say is that the landscape is really cool!

Volax village itself was one of our favourite villages in Tinos. While many of the houses have been restored, others are crumbling or deserted. The owners of one of the shops in Volax have made it their task to write verses of popular Greek songs on the wooden doors and windows.

If you like photography, you should definitely spend some time here. There are also a few places to have a meal or a drink. The locals we spoke to were very friendly, and were very proud when we told them we really liked Tinos!

Agapi Village

Agapi means "Love" in Greek, and is such an interesting place to visit! The whole village is built entirely on a slope, and there are many stairs, steps, arches and other unique architectural features. It is quite maze-like, which is intentional, as they were trying to keep invaders out of the village when they built it originally. At the same time, they always offered hospitality to people who came in peace, hence the name.

When we arrived at Agapi, we saw two or three people out on the narrow streets. Later on, pretty much all the villagers had gathered outside the church! It was really cool to observe the real village life, and it was a surprise to find that the church was Catholic.

We had a great meal in Agapi, at a local café called **Oti Nanai**. The owners are a really friendly couple, and they made the biggest *fourtalia* omelette we've ever seen!

Kambos Village

Not many people would visit Kambos if it wasn't for the newly founded Kostas Tsoklis museum. This is a modern art museum designed by the prolific Greek artist himself, and operating only in summer.

Collections include Tsoklis' work as well as some of his private photographs, files etc. The museum also functions as a cultural centre, organizing workshops, lectures, movie nights and other events.

Visit their website at http://www.tsoclismuseum.gr/en/

Other Villages in Tinos

There are many more villages in Tinos worth visiting. Our advice is to rent a car and set out to explore. Falatados, Mperdemiaros, Dyo Choria, Triantaros, Arnados, Mountados, Karya, Tripotamos, Kalloni, Ktikados, Krokos…

From some point onward, the names might not even be important. Just stop wherever you see a village in Tinos, and we guarantee that you will find something you like about each and every one!

23. Churches and Monasteries in Tinos

From a visitor's point of view, Greece seems to be full of churches. However, few places in Greece have as many churches and chapels as Tinos. You can literally see them everywhere you look, and many of the areas and beaches on the island are named after the nearby church.

Churches in Tinos come in all shapes and sizes, and many materials are in use. You will see simple, white-washed chapels, blue-domed and golden-domed churches, but also imposing, elaborate temples made out of the local marble.

While the official religion in Greece is Greek Orthodox, there are several Catholic churches all around Tinos. This includes monasteries and convents, which is fairly rare in Greece.

Visiting all the churches on the island would take a considerably long time. Besides, there isn't always a way to find any information on opening times – even trying to call doesn't always work! So just wander around the villages, and take a look at the churches - you will discover hundreds! As for the monasteries, here are the most important ones.

Moni Kimiseos Theotokou Kechrovouniou, Arnados

The most important Orthodox monastery in Tinos is close to Arnados village, marked as "Moni Kimiseos Theotokou Kechrovouniou" on Google maps.

It was likely founded around the 10th - 11th century by three sisters from the nearby Tripotamos village, who decided to live close to the small, already existing churches.

Around 120 nuns used to live here at some point, including Agia Pelagia, the nun who had the vision of the Virgin Mary. Today there are about 50 nuns.

Unlike most of the villages in Tinos, the monastery is built like a castle, to protect from invaders, with white-washed walls and streets. You can see the traditional architecture and explore various icons, artefacts and books.

If you are planning to visit, remember to dress appropriately and cover your knees and shoulders. Men should wear long trousers, or they won't be allowed to enter - long shorts are not suitable. If you are in Tinos on 23rd July, there is a special ceremony at the monastery which many people may find interesting to attend.

The monastery's usual opening times are around 7.00-11.30 and 14.30-19.00, though it's best to do some research at the time of your visit.

Note that there is very limited parking nearby, which is often occupied by coaches, so if you have a car you will have to improvise.

Ieras Kardias Catholic Monastery, Exomvourgo (Xombourgo)

In the Exomvourgo settlement, you can visit Ieras Kardias Catholic Monastery, founded by Jesuit monks who came to Tinos during the 17th century. It's an important pilgrimage for Catholics, and one of the most important Catholic monasteries in Greece.

The monastery includes an impressive temple, a library, and several dorms and rooms as well as a restaurant. There is also a memorial created by the famous Tinian sculptor, Ioannis Filippotis.

A big celebration is hosted on the second Sunday in July. Other important masses take place on the first Friday of each month.

Ursulines Convent, Loutra

We found the Ursulines Convent quite a fascinating place to visit. Now a museum, this ex-convent was founded by an Ursuline nun in 1862. It originally functioned as an orphanage and school for local girls from Tinos, but the level of education was so high, that it soon became a popular place to study.

The School reached its peak in the 1910s-30s, when more than 300 students from all around Greece and Asia Minor came to live and study here. Classes included French, music, arts and crafts, sewing and weaving. Soon, the school became very popular among the wealthier families of the time, and many young Greek girls who later became famous were educated here.

Unfortunately, the school closed during WWII and never reached its previous glory afterwards, as locals were leaving Tinos to find work in other places. For a couple of decades, a sewing and weaving school was in operation. Eventually, the School closed down and the last nuns left Loutra in 1985.

Today, the ex-convent operates as a museum, which is run entirely by volunteers. You can see parts of the building, including classrooms, kitchen and restaurant, as well as the temple. The guided tour is very much worth the time, as it explains a lot about life in the convent and it sheds light on life in Tinos a few decades ago.

Opening times are generally 10.30-15.00 on summer weekdays, and you can get in touch at 22830-23414 and 22830-51490.

Jesuits Catholic Monastery, Loutra

The first Catholic monastery to be founded in Tinos, the Jesuits Monastery next to the Ursulines Convent is not open to visitors. Still, there is a library with over 6,000 books dating from the 16th century, and a small folklore museum.

Agia Triada (Holy Trinity) Monastery, close to Agios Fokas

It is unknown when this important orthodox monastery was founded, but it was somewhere between the 11th and the 16th century. Visitors can see the impressive icons and artwork, a library with rare books and manuscripts and a small folk art museum.

During the Ottoman rule, a secret underground school operated within the monastery, which visitors can still see today. A few of the Greek Revolution heroes spent some time here.

24. Beaches in Tinos

Tinos has plenty of lovely places to swim. Whether you want organized beaches or smaller, hidden coves, there will always be a place for you.

Like mentioned previously, you may want to avoid July and August, when the strong winds might make it impossible to relax on the beach. If you are visiting during these times, choose sheltered beaches to spend your days on, or consider getting a hotel with a pool.

Many of the beaches in Tinos are easily accessible by car, and most of the roads that we took to the beaches were paved. There are buses to many of the beaches as well.

Agios Ioannis Porto Beach

Agios Ioannis Porto, to the south of the island, is in a nice location in Tinos. On the map, the semi-circular sheltered bay seems very well protected from the north Meltemi winds. On particularly windy days though, it's not as sheltered as it looks!

Regardless, Agios Ioannis is a beautiful sandy beach and the sea is quite shallow, so it's ideal for families. There are a few trees for shade, as well as a couple of beach bars with loungers and umbrellas.

Agios Sostis Beach

Agios Sostis beach is a large sandy beach to the south of the island. There are a smattering of beach bars, but there are also plenty of quiet spots, and you can also find natural shade.

Fokas Beach

If you want to go swimming close to Chora in Tinos, your best bet is Fokas beach. You can even walk from the town if you feel like it, and there are also several buses going quite frequently during the day.

The beach is fairly mixed, with beach bars, restaurants as well as quieter spots where you can put your towel.

Stavros and Agios Markos Beaches

These two beaches to the west of Chora are swimming spots rather than long, sandy beaches. They are both very close to churches, hence the names. These coves are well-known to locals, and Agios Markos gets busy on very windy days, as it's very well protected from the winds. Parking won't be easy, unless you are happy to park right on the road.

Kionia Beach

Kionia is one of the most popular areas to stay in Tinos, as there are several hotels, rooms to rent and restaurants. The long, sandy beach right in front of the small resort town is quite pretty, and it's a good choice for a non-windy day. Across the sea, you can see Syros.

There is no Greek Island without some Ancient History!

Right next to Kionia beach, you can visit the Kionia archaeological site, for which unfortunately there is very little on-site information. You can see, or rather imagine, the remains of a temple, which was dedicated to Poseidon and his wife Amphitrite.

Apparently, this was the only temple in the Cyclades dedicated to Poseidon, the God of the sea, and people came from all over the wider area of the Mediterranean for a pilgrimage. The temple was built in the 3rd century BC, and was abandoned in the 4th century AD.

Agios Romanos Beach

This sandy beach, looking towards Syros island, might be one of the best sandy beaches in Tinos on a windy day. There are a couple of beach bars and several trees, so you can put your towel down and watch the world go by. There are two roads leading to the beach – both of them are winding and quite narrow, but reasonably easy to drive on.

Kardiani Beaches

There are three beaches below Kardiani village. Agios Petros, Kalivia and Ormos Giannaki are all easily accessible, and quite different from each other.

Agios Petros

This is a long, narrow, secluded beach. There are both pebbles and sand, and it will be difficult to put up an umbrella – so you can either get here early and find some shade, or just enjoy the sun. You will need to walk down a fair few steps to the beach. Bring a mask and snorkel, as there is a shipwreck near the coast that you can explore.]

Kalivia

Another fairly protected sandy beach, which is easily accessible and as such can get quite crowded. Reports on the beach bar's music quality and volume were mixed, so be prepared!

Ormos Giannaki

A protected beach with a mix of sand and pebbles. You can get there by car, or hike from Kardiani village. There are a couple of tavernas and a few places to stay, so it can be a good choice if you want to relax.

Ormos Isternion / Isternia Bay

Isternia bay used to be the port of Tinos in ancient times. Today, there is a short promenade with a few tavernas, restaurants and cafes, and a small beach with a few shaded areas.

Panormos Beaches, close to Pyrgos

On the day you are planning to visit Pyrgos, start your day early and leave some time to visit the three lovely beaches in the area – Agia Thalassa, Ormos Panormou and Rochari. One day is not enough to go to all three, so you are very likely to return!

Ormos Panormou / Panormos Bay

This settlement is a very picturesque little town. There are plenty of restaurants and cafes, as well as a few rooms to let. The local beach is nothing special, but if you decide to base yourself here it's great for a quick swim. Bus routes to Ormos Panormou aren't that frequent – we picked up a couple of hitchhikers on the way, and saw a few more trying to get a lift.

Agia Thalassa / Saint Sea

If you are happy to drive on a narrow dirt road for a couple of kilometres, this beach is probably the best choice on the whole island. It is protected from the wind, there is a beach bar, and there is also plenty of shade.

Despite the dirt road, the beach was actually relatively crowded, by Tinian standards. If you are a good swimmer, you can cross over to the small island nearby, called "Planet".

Rochari beach

Close to Panormos Bay you can find Rochari beach which has a surfers' paradise vibe. There are many trees, so you will most likely be able to find some shade and spend the whole day. There is also a beach bar and even a shower.

Kolimvithra Beach

If we had to vote for our number one beach in Tinos, it would probably be Kolimvithra – we are torn between this one and Agia Thalassa. It's a long sandy beach, with a cool beach bar and a surf school on one side and a large, unspoilt area on the other side. The drive to the beach is amazing, as the whole area is full of reeds.

Santa Margarita Beach

This one is on the east coast, and you can get here through a paved but narrow road. Bring what you will need for the day, as there is no canteen or beach bar.

Lichnaftia Beach

This is a pebbly beach to the east of Tinos, and is quite affected by the Meltemi winds. We wouldn't recommend swimming here when it's windy, as you may actually get hurt. If you drive here, you will need to walk for a few hundred metres to get to the beach.

The location is really quite special, with many reeds and a few houses here and there. There is no canteen or beach bar, so bring everything you need with you. If you look across the sea, you can see Mykonos.

Pachia Ammos Beach

Meaning "fat sand" in Greek, this beach is really a long, wide stretch of sand with many sand dunes. You will need to walk down a path to get to the beach.

25. Outdoor Activities in Tinos

Tinos has a lot to offer in terms of outdoor activities, so there's no excuse for being lazy! Here's a few of the outdoor activities you might like to try.

Hiking in Tinos

Tinos is another lovely Greek island where you can go hiking. There have been recent efforts to clean and maintain the hiking paths in a similar vein to Andros. There is a network of around 150 kms of paths ready to explore on 12 different routes.

The paths combine coastal and inland ways, and have various degrees of difficulty. You will enjoy diverse landscapes, literally hundreds of chapels, and the famous Tinos dovecotes.

As Tinos has dozens of villages worth exploring, you can combine hiking with sightseeing. Obviously, your hike can finish off at a nice village taverna or *kafeneio*! You can find more information about Tinos Trails on their website. https://www.tinostrails.gr/

If you are more into running, you can check out the Tinos Running Experience. This half-marathon has been organized since 2014, and takes place in early June. Check their website for more information. http://tinosrunningexperience.gr/en/

Rock Climbing and Bouldering in Tinos

If you are looking for something more extreme, you can try granite rock climbing and bouldering. The area around Exomvourgo and Volax is a lot more than just a picturesque place.

It may come as a surprise, but the area around Exomvourgo rock in Tinos is the largest boulder centre in Europe. The climbing area was founded over 10 years ago, and has been receiving enthusiastic visitors ever since. There are dozens of rock climbing routes you can enjoy, at different heights and difficulty levels.

To get guidance, rent equipment and for any other information, get in touch with Climb Exomvourgo. This is a local company that specializes in bouldering in Tinos, and can help with accommodation and any information. See http://www.exomvourgo.com/

Watersports and Diving in Tinos

Another island with dozens of beautiful beaches, Tinos is ideal for sports activities and diving. Just remember that the Meltemi season will bring some pretty strong waves!

If you are interested in diving in Tinos, get in touch with Tinos dive centre, who also have instructors in Athens. https://www.facebook.com/thedivecentergr

Due to the strong winds, Tinos is ideal for experienced windsurfers. Other watersports, including kitesurfing, are available on the island. Kolimvithra beach, to the north of the island, has a well-equipped watersports school, Tinos Surf Lessons. You can take classes or just rent equipment. https://www.facebook.com/tinossurf.lessons/

Other beaches that are ideal for watersports are Agios Fokas, Agios Romanos, Kionia and Agios Ioannis Porto. As we were staying near the latter, we can absolutely confirm that it can get quite windy there! While swimming was difficult at times, the beach is ideal for windsurfing.

26. Eating in Tinos

Whether you are a beach bum, an enthusiastic hiker, a religious visitor, a photographer, or just interested in experiencing an off-the-beaten-track Greek island, one thing is certain. You will have to eat while visiting Tinos, and you are likely to have a blast!

Tinos has a wide selection of local cheeses, made exclusively from cow milk, at least in our experience. In fact we saw several cows around the island, but were a little surprised not to find any goat cheese, which is so typical of the Cyclades, while there were goats everywhere in Tinos. The cheeses can be eaten by themselves, and are also used in local pies.

Traditional sausages and meat products are also very popular. If you don't want a proper main course, you can always get a selection of the local cured meats and cheeses. The local sausages are used in the famous *fourtalia* omelettes, which additionally include potatoes and maybe cheese and other vegetables. If you order an omelette make sure you are hungry as they are normally huge!

Another dish we tried in Tinos were the local artichokes, which seem to be a big thing on the island. You can have them marinated, or cured in different ways. If you like savoury flavours, try the local capers as well.

Some of the most popular delicacies from Tinos are the sugar-coated *amygdalota*, super sweet marzipan cakes that are sold all over the island. You will find several types and flavours in many stores around Chora and beyond. Chalaris has some of the best.

Last but not least, Tinos has a couple of wineries, as well as a local beer-brewing company, Nisos. Their Nisos Lager won a prestigious award in the annual European Beer Star competition which happens in Bavaria - it won second place out of 1,613 beers! The brewery is on the way from Chora to Agios Ioannis Porto.

As Tinos has so many villages, there are hundreds of restaurants, tavernas, cafes and kafeneia serving local homemade delicacies. It's worth exploring as many as you can - just pick the ones that seem to stand out.

Prices are very moderate, starting at about 10 euro per person based on two sharing. We were quite happy with every single place that we ate!

Thalassaki, Isternia

Thalassaki (Little Sea) is considered to be one of the best tavernas in Tinos. Using home-grown vegetables and local ingredients, the owner Antonia makes miracles! Try the octopus in the oven, and the aubergine dishes.

Marathia, Agios Fokas

Right on Agios Fokas beach, you can find Marathia taverna, and the adjacent beach bar. The owner Marinos and his two sons are experts in fish and seafood dishes. Be adventurous, and order the dishes you are least familiar with, such as the oven-baked octopus with aubergine.

Katoi, Smardakito

It's worth visiting Smardakito just for this lovely taverna, right on the village's square, next to the church. This is a good place to try hearty traditional Greek dishes such as moussakas, pork or goat in the oven and rooster with traditional pasta.

To Perivoli, Kardiani

A small restaurant with an incredible view towards Giannaki Bay, To Perivoli serves local, home-made dishes made mostly with home-grown ingredients. Zucchinis, aubergines and cheese are everywhere on the menu!

Megalos Kafenes, Pyrgos

This local kafeneio opened on the main square in Pyrgos over a century ago, and there was a major refurbishment in 2014. This is a nice place to have a local *galaktoboureko* dessert or an orange cake and a Greek coffee, under the shade of the old plane tree.

To Agnanti, Ktikados

Another small taverna in the middle of nowhere, To Agnanti has a lovely view and a nice menu which changes often. Don't miss the giant beans, the rabbit stew, and the *fourtalia* omelette.

Oti Nanai, Agapi

Apparently, people come all the way from the other side of Tinos to visit this small, cosy cafe in the shaded square. Run by a young, enthusiastic couple, this is a great place to sit for an hour, and have the biggest *fourtalia* omelette in the Cyclades.

Tip - do not order a second course, one omelette is plenty for a hungry couple! Don't forget your jacket, as even summer evenings can get a bit chilly.

Koutouki tis Elenis, Gafou street, Chora

This is a small traditional restaurant in Chora which opened in 1812 and comes highly recommended. They have an extensive menu with many small dishes, so it's an ideal place to try many local delicacies, including rabbit and dove in red sauce.

27. Nightlife in Tinos

You will have gathered by now that Tinos doesn't exactly scream "nightlife". True, but you can still have a late drink if you know where to go - or you can just stay out late in the local *kafeneio*.

Your best bet if you want a late night is **Village Club** in Chora. Believe it or not, you can go dancing until the early morning hours! **Sivilla Club** right next door is good for drinks and cocktails, accompanied by Greek music.

If you are more into rock music, head to **Koursaros**, one of the oldest bars on the island. You can also have a coffee during the day, with a view of the busy port.

If you have a car or don't mind taking a taxi, **Kaktos bar** in the outskirts of Chora may be a good choice for cocktails, though the prices are on the steep side. You can come here to enjoy the sunset views, and maybe stay longer for a drink. Bring a jacket on windy days!

28. Quick Greek Glossary

Here are 20 Greek words that you are likely to use during your Greek holiday!

CAPS	SMALL	SOUND	MEANING
NAI	ναι	né	yes
OXI	όχι	ohi	no
ΕΥΧΑΡΙΣΤΩ	ευχαριστώ	efharisto	thank you
ΠΑΡΑΚΑΛΩ	παρακαλώ	parakalo	please / you are welcome
ΚΑΛΗΜΕΡΑ	καλημέρα	kalimera	good morning
ΚΑΛΗΣΠΕΡΑ	καλησπέρα	kalispera	good evening
ΚΑΛΗΝΥΧΤΑ	καληνύχτα	kalinihta	good night
ΓΕΙΑ ΣΟΥ	γεια σου	yiassou	hello and goodbye (to one person / informal)
ΓΕΙΑ ΣΑΣ	γεια σας	yiassass	hello and goodbye (to many people / formal)
ΑΝΤΙΟ	αντίο	adio	goodbye
ΜΠΥΡΑ	μπύρα	bira	beer
ΚΡΑΣΙ	κρασί	krassi	wine
ΝΕΡΟ	νερό	nero	water
ΦΑΓΗΤΟ	φαγητό	fagito	food
ΓΕΙΑ ΜΑΣ	γεια μας	yiamass	cheers! (= to our health)
ΤΟΥΑΛΕΤΑ / ΜΠΑΝΙΟ	τουαλέτα / μπάνιο	toualeta / banio	toilet
ΧΑΡΤΙ	χαρτί	harti	toilet paper
ΠΑΡΑΛΙΑ	παραλία	paralia	beach
ΘΑΛΑΣΣΑ	θάλασσα	thalassa	sea
ΦΑΡΜΑΚΕΙΟ	φαρμακείο	farmakio	pharmacy

You can read more about the Greek language at https://realgreekexperiences.com/greek-alphabet

29. About the Authors

Dave Briggs

Dave was born in Northampton in the UK. He's always loved travel, and his first big travel adventure involved buying a car in Australia, and driving around the country for a year.

During 20+ years of self-funded travel since then, he's backpacked through South America, sailed across the Mediterranean, worked as a nightclub bouncer in Sweden, picked grapes in Kefalonia, and travelled as a digital nomad in Asia. He's also completed several long distance bicycle tours, which have included cycling from Alaska to Argentina over 18 months and  cycling from England to Cape Town over 12 months. He also cycled Greece to England - although he calls that one more of a vacation.

These days, Dave spends six months a year in Greece, and the other six months on bike tours and travel adventures. He's the blogger behind Dave's Travel Pages, creating travel guides aimed at making your life easier.

You can check out his blog here:
www.davestravelpages.com

Vanessa Foudouli

Vanessa was born in Athens, Greece. Her first trip abroad was a month-long journey in Europe in an old Citroen 2CV car. At age 27 she moved to London, where she studied and worked for a few years as a social researcher. This was where she first realized that her passion was travelling and meeting people from other cultures.

Her travels have included extended journeys through Europe, South America, the Middle East and Asia, but she has a soft spot for her own country. She enjoys showing people around Athens and Greece, and since 2013 has been running the "Real Greek Experiences" walking  tours, helping visitors discover a hidden, authentic side of Athens.

In 2018, Vanessa started the Real Greek Experiences travel blog for people who want to experience more of the authentic Greece.

You can check out her blog here:
www.realgreekexperiences.com

Made in the USA
Monee, IL
04 June 2023

35239296R00065